WHAT'S SO SPECIA
A
HUNTING ?

Bob Burn-Murdoch

Everything you need to know about England's flattest county,
birthplace of the sandwich, home of King Canute
and Oliver Cromwell, noted for its volcanoes and its
bustards, and for the beauty and sobriety of its inhabitants.

'It would be very difficult to find a more delightful spot
than this in the world' – COBBETT

THE FRIENDS OF THE NORRIS MUSEUM

Published by the Friends of the Norris Museum 1996

ISBN 0 9525900 1 8

The Friends of the Norris Museum
St Ives
Huntingdon
Cambridgeshire PE17 4BX

Printed and bound in Great Britain by The Witley Press, Hunstanton

ACKNOWLEDGEMENTS

The people who have unwittingly helped me to write this book are too many to thank individually, but I am grateful to all those researchers – past and present – who have worked to unravel the mysteries of Huntingdonshire and its history. They are almost all amateurs (in the best sense of that word) – cheerful and eccentric souls whose work forms the basis of all our knowledge of local history.

When this book comes out I know that some of them will say, 'How could you have left out such-and-such?', and others will tell me, 'I suppose you know you're completely wrong about such-and-such.' I forgive them in advance. Huntingdonshire is such a rich field that I can't possibly include all there is to say about it and I know that new research will inevitably make this book out of date even before it comes back from the printers.

The paragraph about Huntingdonshire names on p.29 first appeared in *The Records of Huntingdonshire,* the journal of the Huntingdonshire Local History Society. I am grateful to the editor of the *Records* for permission to reproduce it, and for many other kindnesses.

WHAT'S SO SPECIAL ABOUT HUNTINGDONSHIRE?

One of the things that makes Huntingdonshire special is the fact that it doesn't exist any more. After almost a thousand years (the first authentic use of the word 'Huntingdonshire' was in the Anglo-Saxon Chronicle for A.D. 1011, where it was named as one of several counties overrun by the Danes), Huntingdonshire ceased to exist as an independent county in 1965.

In that year it was merged with the Soke of Peterborough to form the County of Huntingdon and Peterborough. And since 1974 it has had the status of a 'District' within the enlarged county of Cambridgeshire.

But Huntingdonshire lives on. There have been only minor changes to its boundaries over the centuries, and today's Huntingdonshire District is recognizably the same place as the Shire attacked by the Danes in the 11th century. Huntingdonshire's present-day inhabitants are the heirs to a thousand years of extraordinary people and extraordinary events, when the county has often been at the heart of English history.

This book sets out to explain some of the ways in which Huntingdonshire's geography, history and people have made it unique among English counties.

HUNTINGDONSHIRE IS . . .

. . . Small

Huntingdonshire was the third smallest county in England – only Rutland and Middlesex were smaller. The ancient county covered 234,218 acres, but minor boundary changes in Victorian times reduced this slightly to 233,985 acres (94,692 hectares). That's 365 square miles, one square mile for every day of the year.

The present-day Huntingdonshire District is smaller still. When the County of Huntingdon and Peterborough was formed in 1965, Eaton Socon and Eaton Ford were taken out of Bedfordshire and added to it. But when Huntingdonshire and Peterborough were divided into two districts in 1974, as part of an enlarged Cambridgeshire, the new boundary between them was set further south than it had been before. This was to give Peterborough control over its 'Southern Township' in the Ortons, Fletton and Stanground – quiet country villages in the days when Huntingdonshire had extended to the south bank of the Nene, but now busy suburbs of an expanding city.

Including the Eatons but without the Southern Township, Huntingdonshire District now contains 357 square miles.

. . . Flat

Huntingdonshire is the flattest county in England. The highest spot in the county is just over 80 metres above sea level (262 feet). This is a little way uphill from the Three Shires Stone, which marks the point on the road from St Neots to Wellingborough where Huntingdonshire, Bedfordshire and Northamptonshire all meet.

No other county in England has such a low highest point. 'Very flat, Norfolk', says one of the characters in Noel Coward's *Private Lives*. What he meant to say was, 'Very flat, Huntingdonshire.'

. . . in two Hemispheres

Huntingdonshire includes parts of the Eastern and Western Hemispheres. It is one of nine English counties that straddle the Greenwich Meridian. (The others are Yorkshire, Lincolnshire, Cambridgeshire, Hertfordshire, Essex, London, Surrey and Sussex).

The meridian passes a few yards to the east of the central road junction, the Cross, in Somersham; so you enter the Eastern Hemisphere when going to the east half of Somersham village, and when visiting Colne, Bluntisham or Earith.

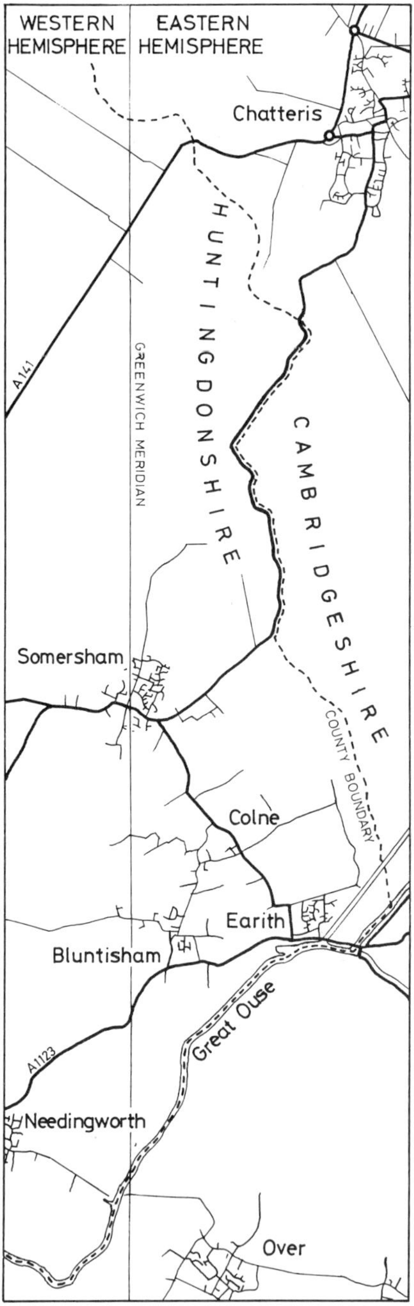

If you like early mornings the Eastern Hemisphere is the part of Huntingdonshire to live in. The sun rises over Earith each day two minutes earlier than it does at Keyston, 20 miles and half a degree of longitude to the west. And Keyston folk see the sun a full twenty minutes earlier than the inhabitants of Penzance in Cornwall.

So just how fast is Huntingdonshire spinning round the earth's axis? That depends where you are. Waresley, right in the south of the county, is spinning eastwards at about 641 miles per hour. If you find that too dizzying, move north. As the earth curves inwards towards the North Pole, its diameter gets steadily smaller the further north you go. Up at placid, slow-moving Stibbington in the northern tip of Huntingdonshire, the distance round the earth's surface is about 200 miles less than it is at Waresley. Stibbington can thus revolve round the earth's axis about eight miles per hour more slowly than Waresley, and still do one complete revolution every 24 hours.

The Greenwich Meridian in Huntingdonshire

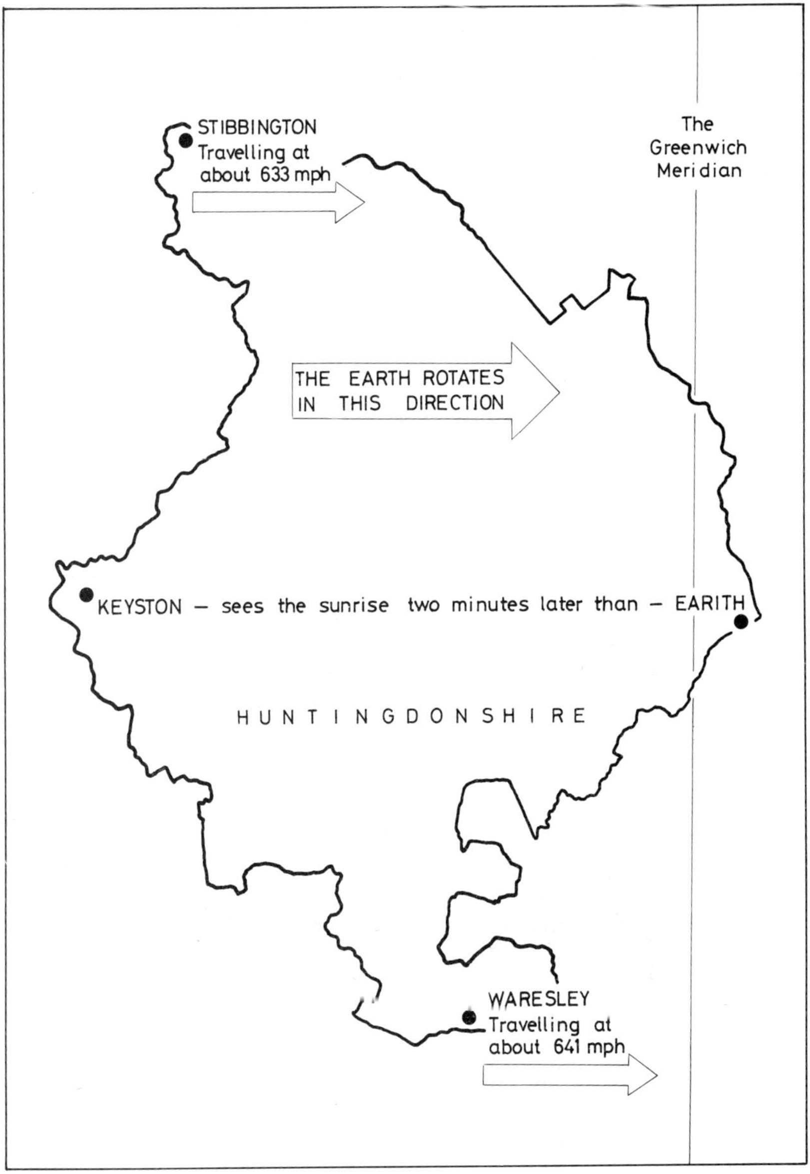

Huntingdonshire and the rotation of the earth

HUNTINGDONSHIRE IS NOTED FOR . . .

. . . its Communications

Huntingdonshire lies on one of the great crossroads of England. Running across the county roughly from west to east is the Great Ouse River, used for transport at least as far back as the Bronze Age, 4000 years ago. The Vikings sailed up it in their longships, and lighters and barges plied the river until the First World War. Nowadays the Ouse has a busy holiday traffic of pleasure boats.

Crossing this east–west artery are two important north–south routes – the Great North Road and the East Coast main railway line.

The Romans built the Great North Road (the present-day A1) and the 'Old North Road' (now the A10 and the A1198). Running north by different routes from London, they join just north of Huntingdon at Alconbury Hill. The road north from that junction, taking the combined traffic of both routes, has always been one of the busiest roads in England. In the middle of the 19th century 44 stage coaches passed along it every day, on their way from London to Boston, Louth, Lincoln, Stamford, Leeds, Newcastle, Hull, York, Edinburgh and Glasgow. The *George* at Huntingdon was said to be the biggest coaching inn outside London, while the village of Stilton had stabling for 300 horses.

Up in the hills in the west of Huntingdonshire was another route. The Bullock Road consisted of country lanes with wide grass verges along which cattle could be driven, away from the bustle and the toll gates of the Great North Road. In the middle of the 18th century, 200,000 cattle entered Huntingdonshire each year along this route.

The East Coast main line, opened through Huntingdonshire in 1850, killed off the stage coaches. But half a century later the motor car appeared on the scene, and then Huntingdonshire became notorious as the setting for the **Buckden Speed Trap**.

The Great North Road bypasses Buckden now, but in those days it ran straight through the village. The Huntingdonshire Constabulary stationed policemen in the main street to time motorists over a measured stretch of road. Anyone going faster than 20 miles per hour was charged with 'driving to the common danger'. In 1906 168 drivers were convicted and fined more than £1200 between them.

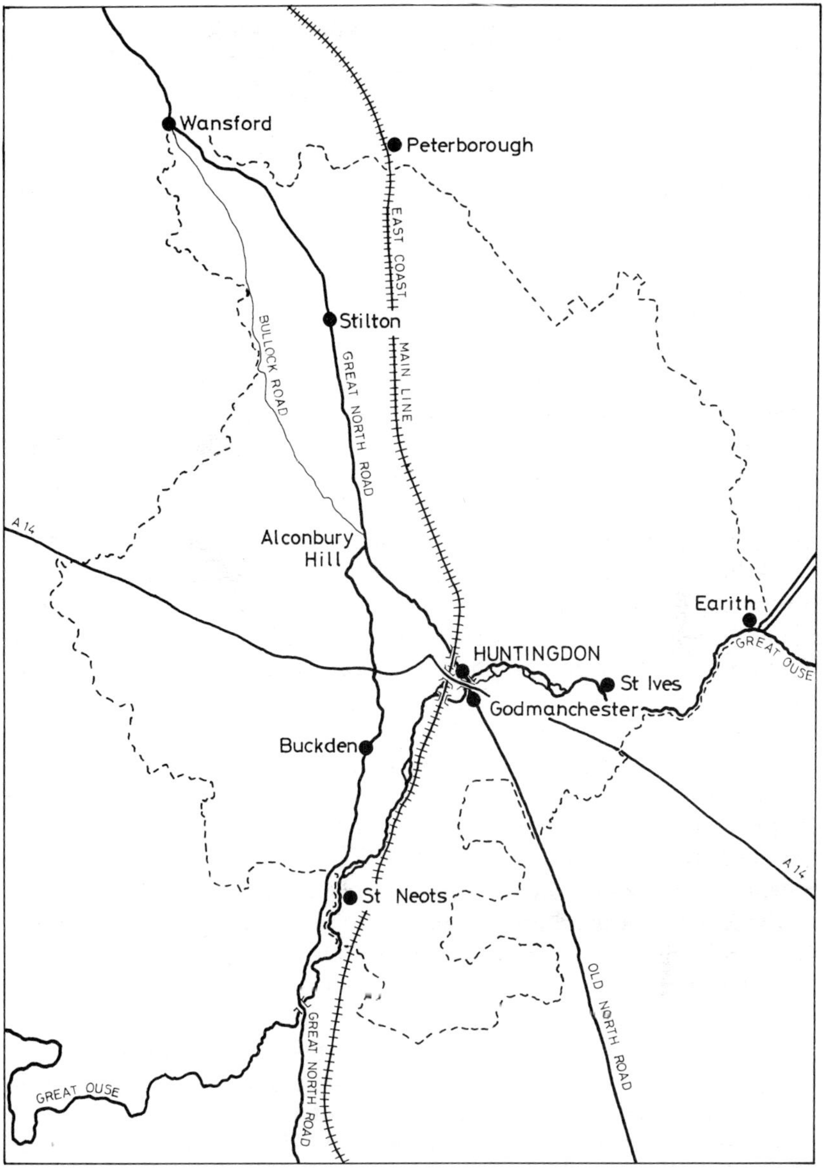

Huntingdonshire at the crossroads: the county and its communications

The effect was noticeable. A motorist's diary of the time includes the entry, 'Very slowly through Hunts., on account of Police'. There was even a campaign to persuade motorists to boycott Huntingdonshire in protest, and avoid driving through it. The idea didn't catch on, and it still hasn't.

The late 20th century brought another major route to Huntingdonshire – and a new means of transport that didn't quite succeed. The major route was the dual-carriageway A14, upgraded in 1994 as part of a road linking the Midlands, the M1 and the East Coast ports. The new means of transport was the Hovertrain.

Officially called the 'Tracked Hovercraft', the prototype Hovertrain was tested at Earith in Huntingdonshire in the early 1970s. This remarkable vehicle floated above a special track, held there by magnetic force. Because it ran above the track instead of on it, the low friction allowed its electric motor to propel it at enormous speeds. The disadvantage was the cost of building the track, raised above the ground on concrete pillars. In 1973, faced with the prospect of having to pay for enough track at Earith to enable the experimental vehicle to reach speeds of 220 miles per hour, the government abandoned the project. Both here and in France – which was also involved in the Hovertrain – more recent efforts have concentrated on building high-speed trains that run on conventional railway tracks.

. . . its Royal Visits

Huntingdonshire's good communications have been a factor in the number of royal visits the county has received – but it hasn't always enjoyed them.

The earliest royal visit probably took place in A.D. 60 or 61, when the Queen of the Iceni tribe – Boudicca, also known as Boadicea – toured various locations in the newly created Roman province of Britain. One of them was probably Godmanchester, then a small town just springing up on the site of the fort the Roman army had built to guard the ford over the River Ouse. Excavations in Roman Godmanchester have revealed a mass of burned remains dating from about the time of Boudicca's rebellion – probably the traces of an Iceni attack.

No less violent was the visit by the Saxon king Edward the Elder. In A.D. 921 he captured Huntingdon from the Danes. (The Romans, invading Britain from the south coast, had built their fort at Godmanchester on the *south* bank of the Ouse. The Danes entered Britain on the east coast and came into Huntingdonshire from the north, so they built their settlement on the *north* bank of the river. The two towns of Huntingdon and Godmanchester have faced each other across the Ouse ever since).

William the Conqueror passed through Huntingdon in 1068, just two years after the Battle of Hastings. He recognized the importance of the river crossing and ordered a royal castle to be built to defend it. (The earthworks can still be seen, behind the Old Bridge Hotel). But in 1173 the garrison of the castle joined a rebellion against William's grandson, Henry II. King Henry came to Huntingdon to take personal charge of the siege, and the castle surrendered the day after he arrived. He ordered it to be demolished.

Henry I, Edward II and Edward III all visited Ramsey Abbey. In 1461, during the Wars of the Roses, the Lancastrian army under Queen Margaret marched through Huntingdon on their way south to the battle of St Albans, and sacked the town.

Queen Elizabeth slept here. Elizabeth I rode up the road from Cambridge (the present-day A14) on 10th August 1564, dined with the bishop of Ely at his house in Fenstanton, and spent the night at Hinchingbrooke House. She knighted her host there, Henry Cromwell.

Huntingdonshire's **Least Appreciative Royal Visitor** was probably Catherine of Aragon, divorced queen of Henry VIII, who thought the local climate was so unhealthy that it would kill her. (She was born in Spain.)

Catherine was taken to the bishop of Lincoln's palace at Buckden in the summer of 1533, a few weeks after her marriage to the king had been declared invalid. She was kept a prisoner there while Henry's courtiers tried to persuade her to acknowledge that she was no longer queen of England – but she stubbornly refused. Next winter she resisted an attempt to take her to the bishop of Ely's palace at Somersham, thinking its location so close to the undrained Fens would make it unhealthy. Instead she was taken to Kimbolton Castle where she died in January 1536. Her body was taken to Peterborough cathedral for burial – her ghost is said to haunt Kimbolton.

Our **Most Appreciative Royal Visitor** was perhaps James I, who stayed at Hinchingbrooke House on his way south from Scotland to take the English throne after the death of Elizabeth I. He was there on the night of 27th April 1603 as the guest of Sir Oliver Cromwell, son of the man Queen Elizabeth had knighted. He is said to have told Sir Oliver that he had been better treated at Hinchingbrooke than at any place he had visited since he left Edinburgh; he certainly created Sir Oliver a Knight of the Bath on his coronation day three months later.

James I visited Hinchingbrooke at least three more times, in 1605, 1616 and 1617.

Our **Quietest Royal Visitor** was his mother. Mary Queen of Scots had been beheaded at Fotheringhay Castle in Northamptonshire in 1587. Like Catherine of Aragon she was buried at Peterborough. When James I came to the throne he had her body brought to London for reburial in Westminster Abbey. It travelled through Huntingdonshire and lay one night in All Saints' Church at Huntingdon.

Perhaps our **Noisiest Royal Visitor** was yet another Stuart, James I's son Charles I. He came to Huntingdon in August 1645 at the head of a force of cavalry – this was after the Cromwell family had sold Hinchingbrooke House to pay off their debts, and had become disillusioned with entertaining royalty.

In the dying days of the Civil War, Charles and his troops attacked Huntingdon from the north on Sunday 24th August. There was a skirmish with a small Roundhead force at the entrance to the town, but no serious resistance. The Royalists then occupied Huntingdon and Godmanchester for two days, and plundered both towns before withdrawing south-westwards on Tuesday 26th August.

A story that the Royalists destroyed several Huntingdon churches during the assault on the town is probably untrue: there are no contemporary accounts of any such thing happening, and one soldier quietly visited four Huntingdon churches during the Royalist occupation, sketching and making notes. Richard Symonds' notebooks are still preserved in the British Library and make no reference to any serious damage.

Any damage to the churches was probably the result of the hard times brought on by the Civil War rather than any deliberate destruction. Certainly All Saints' church tower seems to have needed rebuilding at about this time, and the now vanished churches of St Benedict and St John were largely demolished in the middle of the 17th century. But if there is any truth in the story of the churches' destruction at the hands of Charles I's troops, then his son Charles II must rank as our **Most Insensitive Royal Visitor**. He visited Huntingdon in 1664 and expressed his delight at the 'picturesque ruins' of the town.

Opposite: *Royal visitors to Huntingdonshire: Elizabeth I, Catherine of Aragon, James I, Mary Queen of Scots, Charles I and Charles II*

. . . its Incredible Shrinking Fen

Whittlesey Mere, between the villages of Holme and Yaxley, was the last part of the Huntingdonshire Fens to be drained. Steam pumps emptied it in 1849–53. As the peat of the Mere bed and the nearby Fens began to dry out it shrank rapidly, and sometimes the soil even blew away in strong winds. The result was that the land surface fell very quickly.

To measure the shrinkage, an iron post from the Crystal Palace was driven into the soil not far from the site of the Mere, with its top level with the surface of the ground. 13 feet of the 'Holme Post' is now visible – the ground has shrunk that much in 150 years.

. . . its Volcanoes

In 1966 an aerial survey of the earth's magnetic field detected a disturbance in the magnetism near the disused airfield at Warboys. A borehole was drilled on the spot where the disturbance occurred, and 500 feet below the surface a lump of Dolerite was discovered. Dolerite is a rock formed from the lava flows of volcanoes, and this lump of it was the remains of a volcano that had been extinct for 350 million years. There may be another one under Upwood.

The volcano was reported in local newspapers, and there are still people around who will point out features in the landscape and tell you they are the volcano's crater. Ignore them – they are fooling you or fooling themselves. The crater has long since vanished and all that remains of the Warboys volcano is that mass of dolerite 500 feet under the ground.

. . . its Bustards

The Great Bustard, a gigantic relative of the Lapwing, became extinct in England in about 1850, although there were occasional sightings of visiting Bustards from Europe later in the 19th century. It grew as big as a turkey, and the male birds had strange, bristle-like feathers on each side of their chin. Bustards could run very fast, and they used to be hunted with greyhounds on Newmarket Heath.

The last bustard in Huntingdonshire is said to have been shot at Hilton. It was eaten immediately afterwards.

. . . its Butterfly

Huntingdonshire once had its own butterfly. The Large Copper Butterfly used to breed around Whittlesey Mere – it was only ever found in Britain, and bred only in Huntingdonshire. It became extinct in the

The Great Bustard

The Large Copper Butterfly, male and female

1840s, strangely enough a few years *before* Whittlesey Mere was drained. Burning the reed beds round the Mere where it lived may have caused its extinction.

. . . its Prisoners of War

Prisoner-of-war camps are a familiar concept in our war-torn century. But they were once a novelty, and what may be the world's first purpose-built POW camp was built in Huntingdonshire 200 years ago.

Prisoners of war were traditionally held on converted warships, known as 'hulks', with any overspill being moved to fortresses and ordinary jails. But the length and scale of the Napoleonic Wars proved too much for these methods – more than 120,000 prisoners were brought to this country between 1803 and 1814.

The hulks and fortresses were therefore added to by building three big new prison camps, the first of them at Norman Cross in Huntingdonshire. The later prisons were at Dartmoor and at Perth in Scotland. The Norman Cross camp covered 42 acres and was designed to hold 7000 men, sleeping in hammocks crammed together in big two-storey barrack blocks. The whole camp was built of wood, as a temporary structure: when building work began in 1796, no-one realized that the wars still had nearly 20 years to run.

The first prisoners arrived on 7th April 1797. The camp was emptied in 1802 during the short peace with France, but used again when war resumed in 1803. It was then in continuous use until the defeat of Napoleon in 1814. (His brief return in 1815 did not result in any prisoners being sent to Norman Cross).

The camps at Dartmoor and Perth had been built in stone, and they were used afterwards as ordinary prisons. But the wooden buildings of Norman Cross were demolished in 1816, some of them being sold and re-erected in nearby villages and towns. All that can be seen on the site nowadays are the houses of some of the British officials of the camp, and a surviving section of its outer wall.

Until recently a bronze eagle on a stone column stood beside the Great North Road. It was unveiled in 1914 to mark the centenary of the camp's closure and to commemorate the 1770 prisoners who died at Norman Cross and who lie buried in the unmarked cemetery nearby. The memorial was vandalized in 1990 and the eagle stolen, but there are plans to re-erect it, with a replica of the original eagle, when the new A1(M) motorway is laid out. And several local museums have another memorial of the Norman Cross prisoners in the many beautiful little objects made in carved bone or straw marquetry, by prisoners whiling away their long captivity.

. . . its Pets' Cemetery

Molesworth, in the west of the county, used to be famous for its cemetery for pets. The cemetery opened in 1904 and was run by a Mr Gray whose brother was the keeper of a dogs' cemetery at Victoria Gate in Hyde Park. The Hyde Park cemetery was full up, with about 400 graves, so Mr Gray started his new enterprise in the country. As well as dogs, Molesworth provided the last resting place of cats, birds and monkeys.

The idea was not appreciated by everybody. In 1917 a titled lady living in Portland Square in London hired a taxi to take her dead dog to Molesworth in its coffin. This was at the height of the First World War, and Huntingdon magistrates fined the taxi driver £50 for wasting petrol.

. . . its Cruise Missiles

More recently Molesworth played a part in international affairs. The Second World War air base there became the second site in Britain (after Greenham Common) to house American Cruise missiles in the 1980s. Like Greenham Common, Molesworth drew anti-nuclear protestors to the peace camp outside its gates. Arms limitation agreements with the Soviet Union led to the missiles being withdrawn from the base in 1988, the year after they were installed. Soviet weapons inspectors visited Molesworth to check the base in July 1988.

. . . its Seclusion and Privacy

Huntingdonshire seems to have been the place London folk went to when they wanted to do something in secret. Perhaps it still is.

When the Dutch navy burned the English fleet at Chatham in June 1667, and a Dutch invasion seemed likely, the diarist Samuel Pepys decided that the safest thing he could do with his life savings was to send them down to his father's house at Brampton and bury them in the garden. So he sent his wife and father down to Huntingdonshire with £1300 in gold.

But his troubles were only just beginning. His wife went back to London six days later, on 19th June.

> I and my wife to talk, who did give me so bad an account of her and my father's method in burying of our gold, that made me mad: and she herself is not pleased with it, she believing that my sister knows of it. My father and

> she did it on Sunday, when they were gone to church, in open daylight, in the midst of the garden; where, for aught they knew, many eyes might see them: which put me in such trouble that I was almost mad about it . . . Such was my trouble at this that I fell out with my wife, that though new come to town, I did not sup with her, nor speak to her tonight, but to bed and sleep.

Four months later, in October, Pepys went down to Brampton himself to dig his gold up again. It wasn't easy to find.

> My father and I, with a dark lantern, it being now night, into the garden with my wife, and there went about our great work to dig up my gold. But Lord! What a toss I was for some time in, that they could not justly tell me where it was . . . but by and by poking with a spit, we found it, and then begun with a spud to lift up the ground. But good God! To see how sillily they hid it, not half a foot under ground, and in the sight of the world from a hundred places . . .

Pepys and his clerk spent until two in the morning digging in the garden and washing the gold coins clean in buckets of water. Matters were made worse by his father's deafness, which meant that they had to come

Pepys House at Brampton (photo: Norris Museum)

indoors to discuss where to dig next, in case the neighbours overheard what they were saying. A further session in the garden the next morning, sieving the soil to find more gold, produced all that Pepys thought had been buried, except for about twenty or thirty coins.

> I declared myself very well satisfied, and so indeed I am; . . . and so gives me some kind of content to remember how painful it is sometimes to keep money, as well as to get it.

Strangely enough, a pot of silver coins of the 16th and 17th centuries was found at Pepys' house in Brampton in 1842, hidden in an old wall. Perhaps he didn't recover all his treasure after all.

Someone else who thought Huntingdonshire was a good place for keeping things quiet was Charles James Fox, the 18th-century Whig politician. When he wanted to get married in secret he chose Wyton as the place to do it, and married his mistress Mrs Armitstead there on 28th September 1795. No-one found out for the next seven years.

. . . its Attractiveness

Buckden Towers was a palace of the bishops of Lincoln from the Norman Conquest until Huntingdonshire was transferred to the diocese of Ely in 1837. Thomas Barlow, bishop of Lincoln from 1675 to 1691, spent so much of his time there that he was nicknamed the Bishop of Buckden. He was said never to have set foot in Lincoln cathedral in all his time as its bishop!

William Cobbett, the radical writer of the early 19th century, would have understood Bishop Barlow's point of view. He visited Huntingdon on one of his 'Rural Rides' in 1822, and wrote about it:

> Huntingdon is a very clean and nice place, contains many elegant houses, and the environs are beautiful. Above and below the bridge, under which the Ouse passes, are the most beautiful, and by far the most beautiful, meadows that ever I saw in my life. . . . From the bridge you look across the valleys, first to the west and then to the east; the valleys terminate at the foot of rising ground, well set with trees, from amongst which church spires raise their heads here and there. I think it would be very difficult to find a more delightful spot than this in the world. To my fancy (and every one to his taste) the prospect from this bridge far surpasses that from Richmond Hill. – All that I have yet seen of Huntingdon I like exceedingly. It is one of those pretty, clean, unstenched, unconfined places that tend to lengthen life and make it happy.

SIX THINGS THAT HUNTINGDONSHIRE HAS GIVEN TO THE WORLD

The Sandwich

The sandwich takes its name from the man who invented it, the Fourth Earl of Sandwich (1718–92) of Hinchingbrooke House. The original sandwich was said to be made with salt beef, a favourite food of his. The word was in use by the 1760s.

Sandwich is said to have sat at a gambling table for 24 hours with only a single sandwich (beef between two slices of toast) to sustain him. But his most recent biographer, N. A. M. Rodger, thinks that his addiction to gambling has been exaggerated and that the story is untrue.

When Sandwich's ancestor was created the First Earl of Sandwich in 1660, for helping the Restoration of Charles II, the original warrant was made out with the title 'Earl of Portsmouth' – but this was later changed to 'Earl of Sandwich'. No-one knows why the title was changed. If it hadn't been, we'd all be eating portsmouths instead!

The Fourth Earl of Sandwich

Stilton Cheese

The Queen of English cheeses is named after the Huntingdonshire village of Stilton – but its origins are obscure and controversial.

The earliest description of Stilton cheese was written by Daniel Defoe, author of *Robinson Crusoe*, in his *Tour Through the Whole Island of Great Britain*. This was published in 1725 but described journeys Defoe had made 20 years before, during the reign of Queen Anne. Enjoying Stilton cheese called for a strong stomach in those days:

> Coming south from hence, we passed Stilton, a town famous for cheese, which is called our English Parmesan, and is brought to table with the mites or maggots round it so thick that they bring a spoon with them for you to eat the mites with as you do the cheese.

The cheese is often associated with Cooper Thornhill, a famous landlord of the Bell Inn at Stilton (see below, in the chapter on Huntingdonshire travellers). But Cooper Thornhill didn't take over the Bell until the 1730s, many years after Defoe's visit; so he may have made the cheese famous, but he certainly didn't invent or introduce it.

Controversy also surrounds the question of where the cheese was made. It was certainly sold at Stilton, where the busy stage coach route provided plenty of passing trade, but it is often said that it was only ever made in Leicestershire. It was probably made in Huntingdonshire as well, though: an old man of Stilton who died in the 1770s remembered being sent through the neighbourhood as a boy to collect cream for making the cheese. But when Cooper Thornhill made the cheese popular, he is said to have needed another source of supply, and so sent the recipe to his relatives in Leicestershire and had more cheese made there. A 19th-century clergyman, Rev. Edward Bradley, saw the cheeses being made at Warmington in Northamptonshire, about five miles from Stilton – but the inn landlady who was making them had learned the art in Leicestershire!

We shall probably never know the real origin of Stilton cheese. But its name and its fame derive from Huntingdonshire.

Handel

It would be an exaggeration to claim the music of George Frederick Handel as entirely a Huntingdonshire invention, as he was born in Germany. But the fact that he composed much of his greatest work in England, and that pieces like the *Messiah* remain so popular in this country, is due to the intervention of two Huntingdonshire noblemen.

The First Duke of Manchester, who lived at Kimbolton Castle, helped to persuade Handel to come to England in the first place at the beginning of the 18th century. And in 1784 Manchester's relative the Fourth Earl of Sandwich (of Hinchingbrooke, whom we have just seen inventing the sandwich) organized the celebrations to mark the centenary of Handel's birth. King George III supported the event enthusiastically, and what has been called 'the most important single event in the history of English music during the eighteenth century' took place in Westminster Abbey, with the largest choir and orchestra ever assembled.

The result was to establish Handel, and the *Messiah* in particular, as a central part of English musical tradition. Through all the changes in musical fashion, Handel's popularity in this country has never faltered since Sandwich revived it in 1784.

'Agony Aunts'

Problem-page journalism was the invention of a Huntingdonshire man. John Dunton was born in 1659 in the village of Grafham, where his father was the rector. Rev. Dunton wanted his son to become a clergyman too, but he turned out to be rather stupid at school and so he became a publisher instead, as you might expect.

After some undistinguished years in London as a publisher and bookseller, John Dunton brought out his great idea on 17th March 1690 when he published the first issue of *The Athenian Gazette* (immediately changed to *The Athenian Mercury* because the government was concerned that it might be confused with the official *London Gazette*).

The Athenian Mercury came out weekly at first, then twice a week as the sales soared. It consisted solely of questions sent in by members of the public, printed with the answers given to them by Dunton's panel of experts. The questions were theological, scientific or personal: the first issue, for example, included the questions whether the soul is eternal, whether it is lawful for a man to beat his wife, and why there are spots on the moon. Dunton's experts included Samuel Wesley, father of John Wesley, the founder of Methodism; and Jonathan Swift, author of *Gulliver's Travels*, wrote an ode about the *Mercury*.

The Athenian Mercury was a great success. It ran for seven years and expanded to fill twenty volumes. Questions published in it included:

> Why one Hours Sermon seems longer than two Hours Conversation?
>
> We demand why the English, both Men and Women, are the finest People in the World . . . and yet are the worst Singers in Europe?
>
> Whether to commit Fornication, or eat Black Puddings be a greater sin?
>
> Pray oblige me with the several opinions you have met with concerning the capricious and extravagant humours of women?
>
> Answer – The word *capricious* is used to signify the extravagant humour of most women, because there is no animal they resemble more than a goat . . . Now the cause of a goat's temper is the conformation of the brain, which they say is very like that of a woman.

Dunton blamed Daniel Defoe for the end of his run of success. Defoe started up a similar publication himself, but published his questions and answers more often than Dunton's came out, and flooded the market. Dunton's later publications were less successful and he spent several years in a debtors' prison – possibly dying there, in 1733.

John Dunton

Newsprint

Quite apart from the problem pages, modern newspapers wouldn't exist at all without another Huntingdonshire invention.

In 1804 the watermill at Little Paxton, just outside St Neots, was leased by Henry Fourdrinier and converted to make paper. Until then paper had only been made by hand, but Fourdrinier perfected a machine that could turn out paper in a continuous roll. Patent law was weak in those days and rivals quickly took advantage of Fourdrinier's invention – he went bankrupt in 1808. But it was thanks to him that Fleet Street was later able to use the huge five-mile rolls of paper that make the production of modern mass-circulation newspapers possible.

The Little Paxton Paper Mill continued in business after Fourdrinier had left. It was converted from water to steam power in 1851, and was rebuilt in brick after the old wooden buildings burned down in 1912. It is now operated by Samuel Jones Ltd, no longer making newsprint but still involved in various specialised paper products, in a tradition that now dates back nearly two centuries.

Harvest Festivals

The idea of filling churches with produce and giving thanks for the harvest is not such an ancient tradition as you might think. It was invented by Rev. Piers Claughton, rector of Elton from 1845 to 1859, and the first harvest festival ever held took place in Elton church during his time as rector. Rev. Claughton went on to become a bishop, but was buried in Elton churchyard when he died in 1884.

Elton Parish Church (photo: Norris Museum)

HUNTINGDONSHIRE PEOPLE ARE NOTED FOR . . .

. . . their Beauty

The 'Beautiful Miss Gunnings', the sisters Maria and Elizabeth Gunning, were born at Hemingford Grey Manor House in 1732 and 1733. They lived there until 1741 when the family moved to Ireland. The sisters came to London in 1751 and their beauty created a sensation. Horace Walpole wrote, 'The famous beauties are more talked of than the change in the Ministry,' and 'They make more noise than any one of their predecessors since Helen of Troye; a crowd follows them wherever they walk.'

Both sisters married lords. The Duke of Hamilton was desperately in love with Elizabeth, and when she agreed to marry him he sent immediately for a clergyman and married her at midnight, using the ring from a bed curtain for the wedding ring. That was on St Valentine's Day 1752 and was followed three weeks later by Maria's wedding to the Earl of Coventry.

Elizabeth Gunning

Their happiness was short-lived. Elizabeth's husband died in 1758, and in 1760 Maria died of consumption aged only 29. Her use of white lead on her face to give her a fashionably pale complexion probably didn't help.

By that time Elizabeth had married again, to Colonel John Campbell, heir to the Dukedom of Argyll. He succeeded to the title in 1770, and Elizabeth was Duchess of Argyll until her death in 1790. Her two sons by her first marriage became Dukes of Hamilton one after the other, and two of her sons by her second husband were to succeed him as Dukes of Argyll. So this Hemingford Grey girl was wife to two dukes and mother of four more!

The Gunning sisters were not an isolated case. We learn more about the good looks of Huntingdonshire people from some diary entries made by the Earl of Orford, who travelled through the Fens on a yachting holiday in the summer of 1774. He began his voyage in Norfolk and Cambridgeshire, where the inhabitants were of course much less attractive:

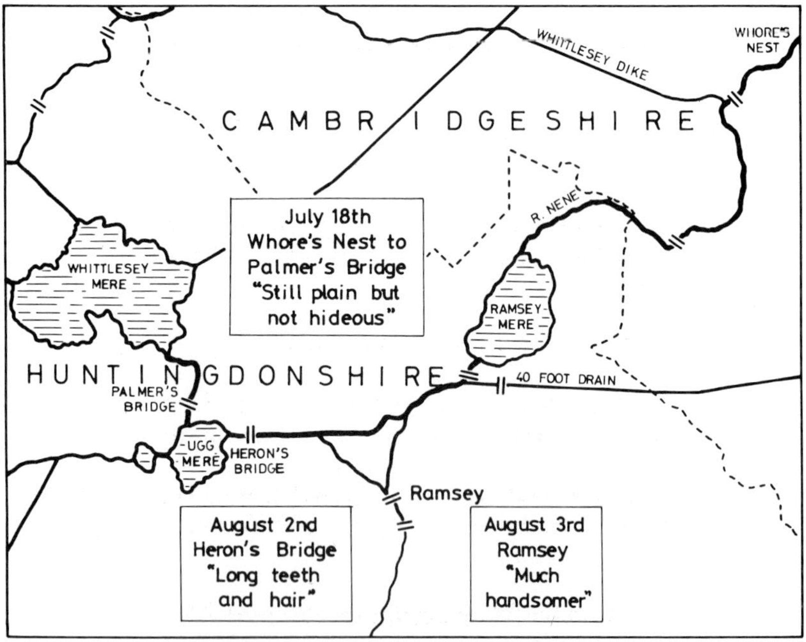

The Earl of Orford's voyage: Huntingdonshire

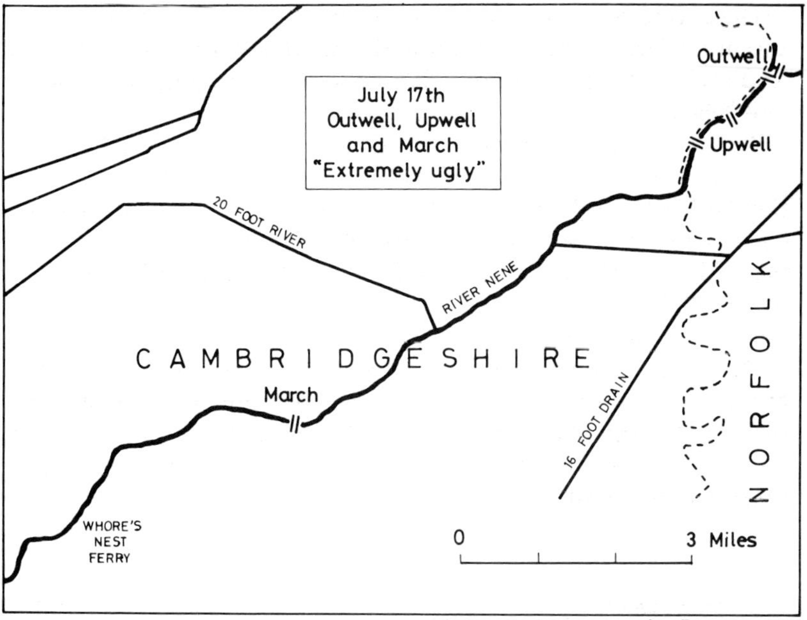

The Earl of Orford's voyage: Norfolk and Cambridgeshire

> Many very old women in Upwell, Outwell, and March: the sex in general extremely ugly.

The next day, sailing south into Huntingdonshire from his overnight mooring at 'Whore's Nest Ferry', Lord Orford began to notice an improvement:

> The sex still plain, but not hideous, as yesterday.

Returning through the same waterways a fortnight later, he was struck by the appearance of a crowd gathered at Heron's Bridge near Ramsey:

> A crowd was assembled near it, and proved the truth of a remark current through this country, that the Ramsey people are famous for long teeth and hair.

But a diary entry on the following day (3rd August 1774) is unequivocal about the charms of Ramsey and its female inhabitants:

> We found the sex much handsomer, and the town better situated and built than any other we had seen in the Fens. The girls had many of them . . . fair hair and good shapes, with expression and life in their countenances; this we attributed to the mixture of French refugee blood settled here in the last century.

Huntingdonshire women are still known for their beauty in the 20th century. Mavis Wright (her real name was Mabel but she changed it) came from a Needingworth family: she was actually born in London, but was brought up in Needingworth and St Ives. She was married twice, to the famous hoaxer Horace de Vere Cole (who fooled the Royal Navy into showing the 'Emperor of Abyssinia' over HMS *Dreadnought*) and to the archaeologist Mortimer Wheeler. Her many lovers included the painter Augustus John. Her career ended in scandal when she wounded another lover, a peer of the realm, with a revolver, and served four months in prison.

Mavis Wright had a military distinction as well. Among her lovers was an RAF Flight Lieutenant who went ashore in one of the first land-

Maria Gunning

ing craft to reach the Normandy beaches on D Day. He set up an RAF Standard on the beach, but before doing so he planted a smaller flag consisting of an item of Mavis's underwear. This must have been one of the first flags to be planted on the invasion beaches.

. . . their Sobriety

In 1894 the *Hunts County News* reported a lecture at Huntingdon in which it was pointed out that Huntingdonshire had the highest number of pubs per head of population for any county in England, and yet had fewer convictions for drunkenness than any county except Wiltshire.

. . . their Names

J. B. Morton, 'Beachcomber' of the *Daily Express,* used to entertain his readers with a mythical *Anthology of Huntingdonshire Cabmen* containing such names as Whackfast, E. W. and Nurthers, P. L.

But truth is stranger than fiction. **John Strokelady** was a chantry priest at Hilton in 1402. **William Ratfoot** lived at Earith at the beginning of the 18th century, though his family later changed their name to Radford. **Original Walter Thong** was a blacksmith in Huntingdon around 1800. **Peter Fullerlove** belied his name in 1849, when he was brought before the Assizes accused of violently assaulting Thomas Simpkin 'by striking him with a bludgeon'. **Ernest William Squelch** became landlord of the Wilkes Head public house at St Ives in 1909. And **Christmas Day** was village postmaster at Bluntisham until his death in 1940.

SOME FAMOUS PEOPLE BORN IN HUNTINGDONSHIRE

Oliver Cromwell

Huntingdonshire's most famous son was born at Huntingdon on 25th April 1599. The house where he was born had been built by his father on the site of a Friary dissolved by Henry VIII. It has been demolished and rebuilt several times since Cromwell's day and nothing remains of the house he was born in except some of the foundations. On the site now is the Cromwell Clinic. The room where Cromwell was born is said to have been above the entrance hall of the present-day building.

One relic of Cromwell's birth that does survive is the record of his baptism. This took place when he was four days old in the parish church of St John. The church too has been demolished since then, but its churchyard can still be seen in Huntingdon High Street. The church's baptisms register is on display at the Cromwell Museum in the Market Hill. Across the entry for Cromwell's baptism someone later wrote 'England's plague for 5 years'.

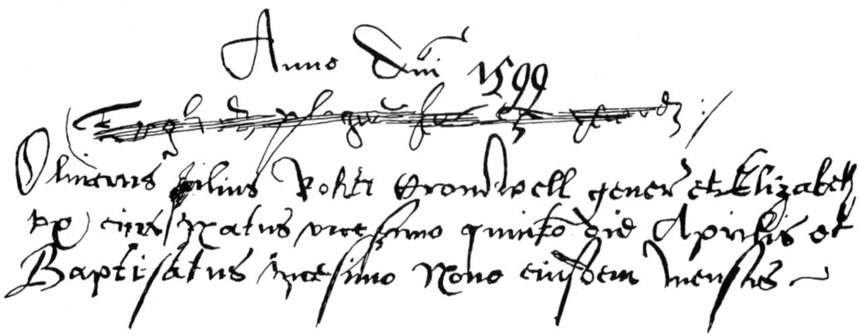

The record of Oliver Cromwell's baptism. Beneath the year ('Anno dni 1599') and above the Latin entry of the baptism ('Olivarius filius Robti Cromwell' etc.) has been written 'England's plague for 5 years' – later crossed out.

Other Huntingdonshire Puritans

Many Huntingdonshire people shared Cromwell's ideas about religion and politics. A pioneer of the movement was **John Howland**, born at Fenstanton in about 1590. He was one of the Pilgrim Fathers who escaped religious restrictions in England by sailing to America in the *Mayflower* in 1620.

Howland almost didn't get there. He was swept overboard in mid-Atlantic but managed to grab a rope and was hauled back to safety. The world would be a different place if his grip had been weaker: his descendants are said to include Winston Churchill, Franklin Roosevelt, Richard Nixon and Gerald Ford.

Other Huntingdonshire Puritans joined Cromwell in the struggle against Charles I. The **Earl of Manchester**, from Kimbolton Castle, was a prominent opponent of the King while Cromwell was still an obscure back-bencher. When Charles I tried to arrest five Members of Parliament in January 1642 – an act that helped to precipitate the Civil War – Cromwell was not included among the five, but Manchester was accused of high treason. He was a general in the Roundhead army in the early years of the Civil War, often with Cromwell serving under him, and was commander of the victorious Parliamentary forces at Marston Moor. But Manchester was no extremist, and began to have misgivings about the way things were going. He withdrew from the War, and later helped to bring about the Restoration of Charles II in 1660.

Stephen Marshall, born at Godmanchester, was a famous puritan preacher who often delivered sermons to Parliament and to the regiments of the Roundhead army. After his death in 1655 he shared with Cromwell the distinction of being buried in Westminster Abbey, and of being dug up again by the mob after the Restoration. Some people felt that his principles were too flexible: the historian Thomas Fuller wrote of him, 'He was of so supple a soul that he brake not a joynt, yea, sprained not a sinew, in all the alteration of times.'

Sir Henry Lawrence of St Ives became a leading puritan politician. He was President of Cromwell's Council in 1654 and was the man who proclaimed Cromwell's son Richard ('Tumbledown Dick') as the second, short-lived Lord Protector after Cromwell's death in 1658.

Valentine Wauton came from Great Staughton, married Cromwell's sister Margaret, and rose to be a colonel in the Parliamentary army. In 1649 he was one of 59 men who signed the death warrant of Charles I. When Charles II returned to the throne in 1660 there was no mercy for the 'regicides' who had put their names to the warrant, but Wauton was one of the few who escaped the consequences. He is said to have fled to Holland and lived there in disguise, working as a gardener until his death in 1661.

Another of Cromwell's brothers-in-law, **John Disbrowe** (or Desborough), was born at Eltisley just outside Huntingdonshire, but played a part in the religious history of our county. He did this by repeatedly rescuing the puritan preacher **Henry Denne**. Denne founded the Baptist churches at Warboys and Fenstanton, but his extreme views often landed him in prison – and on one occasion in front of a firing squad. As a junior officer in the Roundhead army he incited a mutiny in 1649, and was led out into the churchyard at Burford in Oxfordshire to be shot, on 17th May. Three other conspirators were executed, but when it came to Denne's turn he was pardoned by Oliver Cromwell, at Disbrowe's instigation. He returned to his congregations in Huntingdonshire after the Civil War was over, and the 'Particular Baptist' churches at Warboys and Fenstanton are his memorial.

One of the Puritans' greatest enemies also had a connection with Huntingdonshire. **William Laud**, later Charles I's high-church archbishop of Canterbury, was archdeacon of Huntingdon from 1615 to 1621. He was executed by the Parliamentarians in 1645.

The memorial to Sir Robert Cotton in Conington church (photo: Norris Museum)

Sir Robert Cotton

One of an old Huntingdonshire family, Robert Cotton was born at Denton in 1571 and lived at his family home of Conington Castle. He was a great collector of books, manuscripts and coins, and his collection formed the basis of the future British Library. The playwright Ben Jonson was once his guest at Conington.

An interest in constitutional history could be a dangerous hobby in those days, and Sir Robert spent some time in prison for his opposition to the arbitrary rule of Charles I. He died in 1631 and his collections were given to the nation by his great-grandson in 1700.

John Bellingham

John Bellingham was born at St Neots in 1776, the son of a portrait painter also called John, in the house still standing on the corner of Cambridge Street and Huntingdon Street. The family left St Neots in 1777, so the town can't be said to have influenced the young Bellingham very much, which is perhaps just as well.

On 11th May 1812 Bellingham waylaid the Prime Minister in the Lobby of the House of Commons and shot him through the heart.

The assassination of Spencer Perceval

Spencer Perceval thus became the only British Prime Minister to be assassinated – probably the only thing for which he is remembered nowadays. Bellingham had become deranged after his business dealings as a merchant in Russia had gone wrong and he had been imprisoned there for debt. He blamed the British government for not helping him, and this was his revenge. He made no attempt to escape and was hanged a week later.

(Half a century later, another native of Huntingdonshire prevented an assassination. On 6th June 1867 a would-be assassin fired a pistol at the Tsar of Russia and the French Emperor Napoleon III as they rode in a carriage through the streets of Paris. He was thwarted by an aide-de-camp riding forward to put his horse between the man and his intended targets. The pistol ball hit the horse in the head, killing it but saving the lives of the two emperors. The horse was 'Cardigan', bred at Wansford in Huntingdonshire by the landlord of the Haycock Inn. The landlord's name, by coincidence, was Tom Perceval.)

George Gorham

Like John Bellingham, the name of George Gorham is largely forgotten nowadays. But for three years in the middle of the 19th century Rev. Gorham was a famous public figure, and the 'Gorham Controversy' still forms part of the history of the Church of England.

Like Bellingham, George Cornelius Gorham was born at St Neots, on the south side of the Market Square at No. 22. He published a history of the town in 1820, but his life was that of a quiet country clergyman until 1847. In that year he changed parishes, moving from St-Just-in-Penwith, Cornwall, to Brampford Speke in Devon. But the bishop of Exeter refused to admit him to his new parish because he thought that Gorham's theology was unsound. (For the technically minded, Gorham was accused of 'denying unconditional regeneration in baptism'.)

It is hard to believe now what a ferocious controversy could be stirred up by such arcane religious arguments. But three years of fierce disputes followed, with the bishop being supported by the Court of Arches in 1849 but overruled by the Privy Council in 1850. Following this last decision Rev Gorham was at last admitted to his new parish. He died in 1857. More than 50 books were published about the Gorham Controversy, but the disputed piece of doctrine was never settled one way or the other.

Rev. George Gorham

Henry Royce

The co-founder of Rolls Royce was born at Alwalton in 1863, and served his engineering apprenticeship in the Great Northern Railway workshops at Peterborough. He built his first motor car in 1904 and met C. S. Rolls the same year; they founded Rolls Royce in 1906. Sir Henry Royce died a baronet in 1933.

The St Neots Quads

Multiple births are more common nowadays, but the Miles family quadruplets were the first quads in Britain to survive. They were born at home, in a cottage in Eynesbury, in November 1935. Visitors were charged a shilling to peep at the babies through their nursery window.

Huntingdonshire also gave birth to **William of Sawtry**, who on 26th February 1401 gained the melancholy distinction of being the first Lollard to be burned at the stake; to **Nicholas Grimald** (1519–62), a once famous poet born at Leighton Bromswold; and to no less than four Lord Mayors of London: **Sir John Gedney**, Mayor in 1427 and 1447, born at St Neots; **Sir Robert Drope**, also from St Neots, Lord Mayor in 1474; **Sir Ambrose Nicholas**, Mayor in 1576 and born at Needingworth; and **Sir Wolstan Dixie** from Catworth, Lord Mayor in 1585.

SOME FAMOUS PEOPLE WHO HAVE LIVED IN HUNTINGDONSHIRE

King Canute

Tradition has it that Bodsey House near Ramsey was a hunting or fishing lodge of King Canute. A stone in the corner of one of the rooms in the house is said to mark the grave of two of his sons, who drowned while crossing Whittlesey Mere.

Lady Godiva's Son

Domesday Book tells us that the manor of Great Gransden was held before the Norman Conquest by Earl Aelfgar: he died some time between 1062 and 1065. Aelfgar was the son of Earl Leofric of Mercia and Lady Godiva.

Hereward the Wake's Godfather

Also in Domesday Book, Gilbert of Ghent is named as the holder of Fenstanton. The 12th-century biography of Hereward the Wake, *De Gestis Herwardi Saxonis,* identifies Gilbert as Hereward's godfather.

Two Archbishops of Canterbury

Huntingdonshire parishes seem to have been good stepping stones in an ecclesiastical career. **William de Whittlesey**, archbishop of Canterbury from 1369 to 1374, was rector of Fenstanton between 1359 and 1361. And **Thomas Tenison**, rector of Holywell from 1667 to 1681, went on to become archbishop from 1695 to 1715.

The Earl of Worcester

John Tiptoft, created Earl of Worcester in 1449, held the manor of Woolley near Huntingdon. He supported the Yorkists in the Wars of the Roses and so was a marked man when the Lancastrian Henry VI returned to the throne in 1470. The Earl went into hiding in Weybridge Forest near Woolley, but is said to have sent a peasant to buy something for him, foolishly giving the man a coin of greater value than a peasant would be expected to have. Suspicions were aroused and the Earl was discovered hiding up a tree. He was beheaded on Tower Hill in October 1470.

Weybridge Forest has now disappeared and is remembered only in the name of Weybridge Farm, up on the hills overlooking the A1-A14 interchange. Brampton Wood, one of the county's few remaining pieces of ancient woodland, lies a couple of miles to the south.

Henry Montagu

In 1615 Kimbolton Castle was bought by the man who sent Sir Walter Raleigh to the block. Sir Henry Montagu was Lord Chief Justice from 1616 to 1621, and his duties included pronouncing sentence on Raleigh in 1618 – Sir Walter had been condemned to death fifteen years before on very dubious charges.

Montagu's services were plainly well rewarded. In 1620 he paid the Duke of Buckingham the enormous sum of £20,000 to be made Lord High Treasurer, and in 1625 was created first Earl of Manchester by the newly crowned King Charles I. As we have seen, his son the second Earl was not so loyal, taking a prominent part on the Roundhead side in the Civil War.

The Earls and Dukes of Manchester continued to live at Kimbolton Castle until it was sold to become a school in 1950.

Kimbolton Castle (photo: Norris Museum)

Nicholas Ferrar

In 1625 Nicholas Ferrar, a scholar, doctor and Member of Parliament, suddenly abandoned his normal life and moved to the deserted Huntingdonshire hamlet of Little Gidding. He and his family restored the church and set up a religious community together. Ferrar died in 1637 but the community continued until Roundhead soldiers broke it up during the Civil War. Interest in the Ferrars was revived by T. S. Eliot's poem *Little Gidding*, published in 1944. Lines from the poem, inspired by visits to this tiny Huntingdonshire village, form Eliot's epitaph in Westminster Abbey.

A friend of the Ferrars, the poet and hymn writer **George Herbert**, restored the church at Leighton Bromswold, not far from Little Gidding. His influence can still be seen in the way the church interior was laid out, but he never lived in Huntingdonshire.

Mikipher Alphery

Huntingdonshire has produced Lord Mayors of London and Archbishops of Canterbury; Mikipher Alphery was the closest the county came to producing a Tsar of Russia!

Alphery was said to be a Russian prince and a relative of the Tsar, sent to England to avoid dangerous intrigues and quarrels at home in about 1600. He ended up as the rector of the tiny village of Woolley in 1618. But even so far from the Russian court his life was not entirely peaceful, as he found himself caught up in the religious disputes of the English Civil War. In 1643 the Roundheads threw him out of his church (literally – musketeers pulled him out of his pulpit and threw his property out of the rectory; he lived for a week in a tent in the churchyard).

Mikipher Alphery was restored to his living in 1660. He was then over 80 and too old to carry out his duties, so he installed a curate and lived with his son at Hammersmith until his death in 1666.

Samuel Pepys

The famous diarist was born in London but went to school in Huntingdon from about 1640 to 1644, between the ages of seven and eleven. He lived then with his uncle at Brampton, in the house that later became his own property and is still called Pepys House. He went to school at Huntingdon Grammar School, whose most famous Old Boy, Oliver Cromwell, had studied there 30 years before. The building where both Cromwell and Pepys studied is now the Cromwell Museum.

Pepys can hardly have been unaware of the Cromwell connection.

Samuel Pepys

Cromwell had been prominent in local religious and political affairs for many years, and was elected MP for Cambridge in 1640. When Civil War broke out in 1642 he raised a troop of cavalry and rose steadily through the ranks of the Roundhead army. Pepys had returned to London before Huntingdon experienced war at first hand, when King Charles and his cavalry captured the town in August 1645.

Whether it was because of his time at Huntingdon or for some other reason, Pepys certainly favoured the Parliamentary cause when he was a boy. This caused him great disquiet when he met an old school friend in 1660 after the Restoration of Charles II:

> He did remember that I was a great Roundhead when I was a boy, and I was much afraid that he would have remembered the words that I said the day the King was beheaded (that, were I to preach upon him, my text should be – 'The memory of the wicked shall rot').

Pepys had good reason to be anxious. A few months before this meeting he had recorded in his diary that the Assistant Master Shipwright in the Royal Dockyard at Chatham had been dismissed from his post because when he was a child he had spoken disrespectfully of the King! We know from another diary entry that Pepys had actually witnessed the execution of Charles I in 1649, an event that his fellow Huntingdon Old Boy had done so much to bring about. Pepys would have been 15 at the time.

Julius Caesar (but not THE Julius Caesar)

The Caesar family, several of whom were eminent lawyers and judges, bought Great Gransden Hall in the south of the county in 1631. They lived there until 1825. Several members of the family were given the christian name 'Julius', including one who rose to become a Privy Councillor and Master of the Rolls, and died as 'Sir Julius Caesar' in 1636.

Sir Julius never lived at Great Gransden, however. Among the Caesars who lived at Gransden Hall there was only one Julius, who was born in 1703 but died before he came of age. He had an elder sister called Julia Caesar.

John Dryden (but not THE John Dryden)

The poet John Dryden was born just outside Huntingdonshire, at Aldwincle in Northamptonshire. But he had a cousin, also called John Dryden, who lived at Chesterton in Huntingdonshire, and we know that the poet came to visit him there. Dryden wrote an ode to his cousin, beginning:

> How Bless'd is He, who leads a Country Life,
> Unvex'd with anxious Cares, and void of Strife!

Dryden also wrote an epitaph for another Huntingdonshire relative. Perhaps he was having an off day when he wrote it, but it doesn't rank with his greatest work. Dryden's sister married Dr John Lawton of Catworth, who already had a family by his first wife and who had another son by Dryden's sister – her only child, who died before she did. Dryden wrote:

> Stay Stranger stay and drop one Tear
> She allways weeps that layd him Here
> And will do, till her Race is Run
> His Fathers fifth, her only Son.

William Cowper

The poet William Cowper (usually pronounced 'Cooper') lived in Huntingdon from 1765 to 1767. He was the author of many hymns, and of the comic ballad *John Gilpin*. He moved to Huntingdon from a private asylum at St Albans, where he had been treated for insanity, and took lodgings in the High Street. A few months later he moved in with Rev Morley Unwin and his family, and lived with them in the house still called Cowper House, opposite St Mary's church.

Cowper's happy time at Huntingdon came to an end with the death of Rev Unwin after a fall from his horse in July 1767. Cowper and Mrs Unwin then moved to Olney in Buckinghamshire, attracted there by the reputation of its curate, John Newton. Newton, the slave-trader turned clergyman, is best known nowadays as the writer of the hymn *Amazing Grace*. But his gloomy view of religion was the last thing Cowper needed, and the poet was insane again by the beginning of 1773.

William Cowper

Newton left Olney for London in 1779 and Cowper recovered immediately.

Cowper recorded a memory of his time in Huntingdon in a letter he wrote to Newton in 1785:

> I remember a good man at Huntingdon, who, I doubt not, is now with God, and he also kept a Diary. After his death, through the neglect or foolish wantonness of his executors, it came abroad for the amusement of his neighbours. All the town saw it, and all the town found it highly diverting. It contained . . . a faithful record of all his deliverances from wind (for he was much troubled with flatulence), by whatever vent it escaped him; together with pious acknowledgements of the mercy. There is certainly a call for gratitude, whatsoever benefit we receive; . . . but it would have been as well if . . . my old friend had [not] recorded his eructations.

Other Writers

Many other authors and poets have lived in Huntingdonshire. **Laurence Sterne**, author of *Tristram Shandy* and *A Sentimental Journey*, was ordained a clergyman at Buckden in 1736.

George Borrow, author of *The Romany Rye* and *Wild Wales*, spent a year of his childhood in Huntingdonshire when his father, an army officer, was posted to the garrison of the Norman Cross prisoner-of-war camp in 1810–11. It was while roaming in the countryside round the prison camp that Borrow first met the gypsies who were to cast such a spell over his imagination.

The hymn writer **Frederick Faber** was rector of Elton from 1843 to 1845. During his time there he was converted to the Roman Catholic church, and he later founded the Brompton Oratory.

Dorothy Sayers, creator of the detective Lord Peter Wimsey, was brought up in Bluntisham. Her father was rector there from 1897 (when Dorothy was four) until 1917.

The poet and playwright **John Drinkwater** lived at Pepys House in Brampton, and wrote a book there about Pepys which was published in 1930.

The author **Beverley Nichols** lived in a cottage at Glatton in the 1930s and wrote his first book about gardening there. A fictionalised version of the village and his house appeared in his books *Down the Garden Path, A Thatched Roof* and *A Village in a Valley*.

The children's writer **Lucy Boston** bought the Manor House at Hemingford Grey in the late 1930s and lived there for the rest of her life. After lovingly restoring it and planting its garden, she immortalised it as 'Green Knowe' in a series of books for children. A remarkable character, Lucy also made beautiful patchworks and entertained RAF Wyton bomber crews to musical evenings at the Manor House during the war. Her eccentricities led to her being reported to the authorities as a spy by – so she said – every other person in the village.

John Oxlee

Rev John Oxlee was rector of Molesworth from 1836 until his death in 1854. He was a great linguist and was said to have a knowledge 'more or less extensive' of 120 languages and dialects. There was perhaps not much else to do in Molesworth in those days.

SOME FAMOUS (AND NOT SO FAMOUS) PEOPLE WHO HAVE DIED IN HUNTINGDONSHIRE

Saint Neot

St Neot didn't actually die in Huntingdonshire, but he spent some time here after his death. His bones were originally kept in a shrine at St Neots in Cornwall, but were moved to a monastery in Eynesbury in Huntingdonshire in the reign of King Edgar, in the 970s. The monastery then became known as 'St Neot's Priory', and the name St Neots was given to the town that grew up around it.

Why were the bones moved? The traditional story is that the saint appeared in a vision to the warden of his shrine in Cornwall and complained of being neglected by the local people. He then ordered the warden to take his bones to Huntingdonshire. But Rev Gorham, creator of the Gorham Controversy (see p.34) and author of a History of St Neots published in 1820, took the more cynical view that the warden had been bribed to steal the relics.

Whatever the true explanation, St Neot may not have stayed in Huntingdonshire for very long. There is a tradition that when St Neots Priory was destroyed by the Danes in A.D. 1010, the monks sent the saint's bones to the monastery at Crowland in Lincolnshire for safe keeping. The Crowland monks later claimed that they had kept St Neot's bones and sent someone else's back to St Neots instead.

(The reason why there is a 'St Ives' in both Huntingdonshire and Cornwall is completely different. The Huntingdonshire town is named after St Ivo, supposedly a Persian bishop who died there in the Dark Ages. But the Cornish St Ives was named after the Celtic Saint Ia or Hya, and was known as 'St Ie's' until the 16th century. It then began to be called 'St Ives', perhaps by people who had heard of the Huntingdonshire town, or possibly by confusion with the French saints Ivo or Yves.)

The Witches of Warboys

Alice and John Samuel and their daughter Agnes were hanged at Huntingdon in 1593 after being accused of bewitching some of their neighbours in the village of Warboys. One of their alleged victims died – she was Lady Cromwell, aunt of the future Lord Protector.

Half a century later, in 1646, eight men and women from the villages of Catworth, Molesworth, Keyston and Bythorn were condemned for witchcraft by the Huntingdonshire justices, and presumably hanged. This was during the witch hunt unleashed by the 'Witchfinder General', Matthew Hopkins. In this atmosphere of hysterical persecution, it is worth remembering that a Huntingdonshire man stood up against Hopkins. John Gaul, the vicar of Great Staughton, published a book denouncing the witchfinder's methods of extracting confessions. Hopkins threatened to pay a special visit to Great Staughton to look for witches there, but his threat was an empty one. Gaul remained vicar there until his death in 1687, 40 years after Hopkins (according to legend) had himself been executed as a witch.

James Nayler

Nayler, a pioneer of the Quaker movement, died in Huntingdonshire in 1660. Walking along the Great North Road on his way home to his wife and family in Yorkshire, he was robbed and left tied up in a field. He was rescued and taken to a friend's house at Holme, but died soon afterwards aged only 44. He was buried in a Quaker burial ground at Kings Ripton, later planted as an orchard.

The orchard at Kings Ripton was the peaceful end to a life of persecution. Quakers were shown no mercy in those days, and Nayler bore on his forehead a letter 'B' for 'blasphemer', branded there by order of Parliament in 1656. At the same time he had been whipped through the streets of London, receiving 310 lashes. He would have received 311 but the hangman tripped and delivered the last stroke onto his own hand, 'which hurt him much'.

Oliver Cromwell's Cousins

The Cromwell family, of whom Oliver Cromwell was the most famous member, originally had the surname Williams. They changed it to Cromwell in the 16th century to draw attention to their relationship to Henry VIII's minister Thomas Cromwell. (Richard Williams, who made the change in the surname, was Thomas Cromwell's nephew). But after the death of Oliver Cromwell and the return of the Stuart kings, drawing attention to themselves didn't seem such a good idea any more, and several Cromwells changed their name back to Williams again.

One of those who made the change was Oliver's cousin Henry Cromwell, of Bodsey House near Ramsey. He had been a Member of Parliament while Oliver was in power, and had the courage to speak out

James Nayler

against the rule of the Major-Generals, England's only experiment with a military dictatorship. In 1660 he supported the restoration of Charles II and it was then that he changed his name back to Williams.

Henry Williams died of politics. He threw himself into an election campaign in 1673 with such vigour that when he heard his candidate had lost, as he was sitting drinking with friends, he fell out of his chair and died immediately.

Another of Oliver Cromwell's cousins kept his surname but died almost as suddenly. William Cromwell died at Ramsey of the Plague in February 1666. He was said to have caught the disease by wearing a coat made from cloth brought from London, where the Plague was raging.

The tailor who made the coat died too, with all his family, and 180 other inhabitants of Ramsey.

John Pyott

John Pyott was a nonconformist minister at Ramsey who died in March 1735. In those days dissenters often had no burial grounds at their own chapels and had to be buried at the parish church, an institution they had spent their lives attacking. The entry in the Ramsey parish church register for Pyott's burial has an addition, in different handwriting:

'John Pyott. Now Quiet'

Capability Brown

Like St Neot, the famous landscape gardener Lancelot 'Capability' Brown did not die in Huntingdonshire, but he was buried here. He had bought the manor of Fenstanton and Hilton in 1768 and died in 1783. He and his wife lie in unmarked graves outside the north wall of the chancel of Fenstanton parish church, with a memorial inside the building.

Lightning at Great Staughton

An inscription on the outside of the church tower at Great Staughton records the following:

> In the Belfry of this Church, John Chapman aged 40, William Goosey aged 15, Charles Favel aged 11, were instantaneously killed by a flash of lightning on 17th July 1787 at about 4 in the afternoon, in the presence of several persons whose lives were miraculously preserved.

HUNTINGDONSHIRE'S REMARKABLE TRAVELLERS

Cooper Thornhill

Our small county has been the home of some remarkable travellers. For sheer speed it would be hard to beat Cooper Thornhill, landlord of the Bell Inn at Stilton. On 29th April 1745 he bet that between sunrise and sunset he could ride from Stilton to London, back to Stilton and then back again to London – a distance of 213 miles in 15 hours.

He managed it easily. Different accounts give his time for the distance as either 11 hours 33 minutes or 12 hours 17 minutes. Either way Cooper Thornhill won his bet (either 500 guineas or 590 guineas – accounts differ here too) and the nickname 'The Stilton Hero'. All this in spite of the people of St Neots, who are said to have mostly bet against him and who tried to hold him up by barricading the road – but they weren't quick enough, and Thornhill galloped past before they could stop him!

(Dick Turpin is said to have ridden the 200 miles from London to York in ten hours, which would have been quicker than Thornhill's feat; but there is no good evidence for this. Turpin was born in Essex and so can't be regarded as so reliable as a Huntingdonshire man. In any case, the famous ride to York was probably actually made by another highwayman, 'Swift John' Nevison, who took nearly 16 hours to cover the distance when establishing an alibi in 1676.)

Richard Walter

Great Staughton church has a memorial to Rev. Richard Walter, who died there in 1785. As a young man, Walter left his comfortable Fellowship at a Cambridge college to become chaplain on board HMS *Centurion*, flagship of Commodore George Anson. Anson's squadron of six ships sailed from England in September 1740 to attack the Spanish in the Pacific. Four years later Anson returned home with just a single ship, having sailed right round the world – but that surviving ship had on board £500,000 in Spanish treasure.

Walter, his health broken by the hardships of the voyage, had to be sent home from Macao in China after two years. But he was appointed chaplain of Portsmouth Dockyard and later edited Anson's journal of the voyage.

The Bell Inn at Stilton, in the early years of this century (photo: Norris Museum)

Philip Tillard

Philip Tillard of Stukeley Hall, Great Stukeley, was a student at Oxford when he toured Europe in the summer and autumn of 1833. His diaries of the journey show him to have been the kind of traveller for which England has always been famous. Here are some extracts:

> I cannot say, at present, . . . that I am much prepossessed in favour of the Belgian men; there is something uncouth, and almost uncivilised about them.
>
> The Peasantry in the Duchy of Baden are intolerably dirty.
>
> I never met with such an infamous set as these Italians are. I called the Swiss cheats, but they *only* try to make unreasonable bargains &c – but these fellows will not adhere to a bargain . . . The men have a thorough savage appearance . . . These Italians have no idea of *comfort*, & in fact foreigners in general have but very limited notions on that point . . . Foreigners affect to laugh at us, but only because they are ignorant or jealous.
>
> Rome is a superb city, yet in no point of view does it equal such towns as Liverpool &c (barring, of course, its Ruins & St Peter's).
>
> There are numbers of English here:– it is *impossible* to mistake them: I may be bigotted, but there is a something (foreigners call it *pride*) about the air & general appearance of John Bull, which certainly makes him look the Gentleman far more than a foreigner does.
>
> The view [from the top of St Peter's], of course, is not to be compared with that from the top of St Paul's, as from the former you have only Rome.
>
> The French women hideously ugly – but *certainly* prettier *figures* than les Anglaises.
>
> A little care . . . is necessary in this management of the Doganieri [i.e. customs officers] for although on the Continent they never refuse a fee if properly offered, yet the Tourist must be careful not to shock them by offering the fee in too open a manner.

But Tillard ends his diary on an optimistic note:

> There are many more Hints which might be given, but the change that is every day taking place, & which must gradually increase the civilisation of foreigners will render them of little use. English manners, and Anglified Notions are daily spreading throughout Europe, & the Traveller will find that even Italians have now *some* notion of that Word, till lately so peculiar to England, '*Comfort*'.

Mrs Duberly

Great Staughton, where Richard Walter lies buried, can also claim a connection with one of Huntingdonshire's remarkable women travellers. For 200 years Great Staughton has been the home of the Duberly family, living first at Gaynes Hall (now part of Littlehey Prison) and more recently at Place House. In 1854 Captain Henry Duberly sailed for the Crimea with the 8th Hussars. His wife flouted convention and went with him.

Mrs Duberly sailed with the army to Bulgaria, but there Lord Lucan, commander in chief of the cavalry, refused to let her go any further. Disguised as a Turkish woman she had herself smuggled on board one of the transport ships and reached the Crimea. On the morning of 25th October 1854 her husband sent a note from headquarters to the ship in Balaclava Harbour where she was living, to warn her that battle was about to be joined. She galloped her horse up to headquarters and so was able to witness the Battle of Balaclava and the doomed Charge of the Light Brigade. She published the journal of her adventures the following year.

Isabella Bird

An even more remarkable woman traveller was Isabella Bird of Wyton. Less than five feet tall and in poor health with a spinal complaint, she lived with her clergyman father at Wyton rectory. At the age of 23 she was sent to America for her health and discovered that travelling really was good for her.

She never looked back. After her father's death she went to America again and then began a string of journeys to far-flung parts of the world, writing about her travels in a series of books. She went to Hawaii and Japan and climbed the Rocky Mountains with only a guide for company, but returned to England after catching a fever in Egypt. She recovered and married, but was widowed after only five years and set out on her travels again. She went to China and Tibet and was the first English woman to cross Persia, Kurdistan and Armenia. Elected the first woman member of the Royal Geographical Society, she travelled through Morocco at the age of 69, just three years before her death.

Captain Scott's Expedition

With so many Huntingdonshire people travelling almost to the ends of the earth, it seems appropriate that the county has a connection with some travellers who really did go to the end of the earth.

In July 1901 the parish church at Hilton was the setting for the wedding of Oriana Souper, whose family lived in the village, to Edward Wilson, a distinguished doctor and scientist. Ten years later, Wilson was one of Captain Scott's companions on his fatal expedition to the South Pole. They reached the Pole on 18th January 1912 to find that Amundsen had beaten them to it. Wilson, Scott and Bowers died together in their tent not long afterwards. Scott wrote in a last letter to Mrs Wilson that her husband 'died as he lived, a brave, true man – the best of comrades and staunchest of friends.'

Another link between Huntingdonshire and Captain Scott is provided by the War Memorial in Huntingdon's Market Hill. The bronze statue, usually called the 'Thinking Soldier', was sculpted by Captain Scott's widow. It was unveiled on Armistice Day 1923.

The Thinking Soldier at Huntingdon

HUNTINGDONSHIRE'S REMARKABLE MEMBERS OF PARLIAMENT

Edward Wortley Montagu

Montagu was Member of Parliament for Huntingdonshire between 1747 and 1754. His mother is said to have described him as an excellent linguist and a thorough liar, but most historians take the simpler view that he was more or less insane. His remarkable appearance was helped by the fact that he wore a wig made of iron wire. Most of his time as MP for Huntingdonshire he spent in France, including a spell in prison in Paris for cheating at cards.

Edward Wortley Montagu wearing Turkish costume

Lord John Russell

Russell, a Prime Minister and architect of the Great Reform Bill, was MP for Huntingdonshire from 1820 to 1826. (His title of 'Lord John' was a courtesy title, given to him as the son of the Duke of Bedford, but he was not a peer of the realm and was entitled to sit in the House of

Commons). The Huntingdonshire electorate threw him out in the 1826 elections and he never stood for the county again: it was as MP for Tavistock that he proposed the Reform Bill in 1831–2 and as MP for the City of London that he was Prime Minister from 1846 to 1852.

John Major

But we got our Prime Minister in the end. John Major, whose Huntingdon constituency more or less coincides with the old Huntingdonshire seat, became Prime Minister in November 1990.

HUNTINGDONSHIRE'S MILITARY TRADITIONS

The Army

Huntingdonshire once had its own regiment, the 31st Foot. It began life as a regiment of Marines in 1702, and took part in the capture of Gibraltar in 1704 and the battles of Dettingen (1743) and Fontenoy (1745). It became the Huntingdonshire Regiment in 1782, and it was with this title that it fought under the Duke of Wellington in the Peninsular War, and in Afghanistan, the Crimea and China.

In 1881 the Regiment lost its Huntingdonshire connection and became the First Battalion of the East Surrey Regiment instead. Since then there have been further amalgamations and the unit is now part of the Queen's Regiment, whose regimental music still includes a tune called 'The Huntingdonshire March'.

Meanwhile, the First Huntingdonshire Rifle Volunteer Corps had established a tradition of its own. The Volunteers were similar to today's Territorials – part-time soldiers who could be mobilized in the event of an invasion or emergency.

Being Huntingdonshire men, the Rifle Volunteers had some unique local talents. In hard winter weather in December 1870, forty members of the Corps held a skating parade on the flooded and frozen river meadows at Hartford near Huntingdon. They performed various drills on skates, starting and stopping with great precision on the word of command, and even forming squares to resist an imaginary attack by cavalry.

The forty soldiers who put on this display represented more than half the total strength of the Corps – a tribute to the skating prowess of Huntingdonshire people in the hard winters of Victorian times.

The Navy

The Huntingdonshire villages of Glatton and Holme, in the north of the county, have their own naval tradition. A Chatham shipbuilder named Wells bought a large estate in the two villages in 1752, and later named a ship he built the *Glatton*. The *Glatton* was bought by the government in 1795 and commissioned into the Royal Navy as *HMS Glatton,* a 56-gun frigate. The following year, commanded by Captain Trollope, the *Glatton* single-handedly engaged a squadron of six French frigates and fought them for twelve hours. The action was broken off when darkness

The Skating Parade of the First Huntingdonshire Rifle Volunteers

fell, but Trollope carried out repairs during the night and attacked again in the morning. The French ships fled and the *Glatton* pursued them to the Dutch port of Vlissingen before turning back to Yarmouth to refit. Trollope's crew had only two men wounded, while the French had seventy killed or wounded and one of their frigates sank at Vlissingen. This was despite the fact that the largest French ship was 300 tons larger than the *Glatton*.

After this episode the name *HMS Glatton* was preserved in the Royal Navy, and an armoured warship of the same name was built in 1868.

Meanwhile the Wells family stayed in their Huntingdonshire estate, living at Holme House (later rebuilt as Holmewood House). They kept their connection with the sea as well. Thomas Wells, the son of the shipbuilder who had first bought the property, reached the rank of Vice Admiral before his death in 1811.

Vice Admiral Wells seems to have been a curious character. He wrote and published two poems in which he described his bad relations with the villagers of Holme – they had lately cut down and burned the avenue of trees leading to Holme House, and had also hung the Admiral in effigy:

> Me they suspended on the fatal Tree,
> With serious, sad Solemnity;
> (Would I could tie them to the Stocks and lash 'em).

But Admiral Wells consoled himself with the thought of the two outside privies he had built, one in front of his windows at Holme House and the other on the shore of Whittlesey Mere:

> In this I ev'ry Day
> With fervent Zeal and humble Rev'rence pray,
> And costly Off'rings leave behind.

The Air Force

In the Second World War, the Royal Air Force's first sortie over Germany was flown from RAF Wyton. A Blenheim of 139 Squadron took off one minute after the war began, at 12.01 on 3rd September 1939, and flew a reconnaissance mission over the port of Wilhelmshaven. Intense cold froze the radio and it wasn't until the aircraft returned to Wyton that news of German warships in the port could be sent to Bomber Command – too late for an attack to be launched that day.

The following year, in June 1940, an Anson flown from Wyton detected for the first time the radio beams that the Luftwaffe was using to guide its bombers to targets in Britain. This was a crucial discovery in the British defence against the German threat from the air. Later in the war Wyton was the headquarters of Bomber Command's Pathfinder Force, using similar electronic aids to spearhead the RAF's offensive against German cities.

HUNTINGDONSHIRE SUPERLATIVES

The Biggest Meadow

Portholme, the low-lying island between Huntingdon and Godmanchester, is often said to be **the biggest meadow in England**. In *The King's England* in 1939, Arthur Mee called it the largest meadow in Europe, or alternatively 'the widest stretch of grass in any town without a tree'. The whole island covers a little over 300 acres, although it is nowadays divided into two by the railway line running across it.

We must bear in mind that a 'meadow' strictly speaking means an area of grass that is mown for hay. There may be larger areas of grassland in England, and indeed in Europe, but Portholme – fertilised by the winter floods of the Ouse each year to give a rich crop of hay – is in a special category.

The Biggest Lake

The last part of the Huntingdonshire Fens to be drained was Whittlesey Mere, extending over 1600 acres – 2½ square miles – of the parishes of Holme and Yaxley. It may have been even bigger before the drainage of the Fens began in the 17th century, but there are no accurate maps from that far back that would tell us its true area. But at 1600 acres the Mere was still **the biggest English lake outside the Lake District**. (The largest of the Norfolk Broads, Breydon Water, is only 1200 acres).

Whittlesey Mere was drained by steam pumps between 1849 and 1853. Various objects were found on the lake bed that must have been lost from boats crossing the Mere. They included two magnificent pieces of church plate made of silver-gilt: a boat-shaped container for incense, and a censer in which incense would be burned during church services. Rams' heads on the ends of the boat suggest these objects came from Ramsey Abbey. The boat also has Tudor roses on its top, suggesting it was made not long before Ramsey Abbey was closed down by Henry VIII in 1539 – how did these pieces of Ramsey Abbey treasure come to end up on the bed of Whittlesey Mere? (They are now in the Victoria and Albert Museum.)

Also found on the drained Mere bed were four massive blocks of limestone, which were probably being ferried to Ramsey Abbey for building work there; and the skeleton of a grampus (a kind of whale) that must have swum too far inland when the Mere was still connected

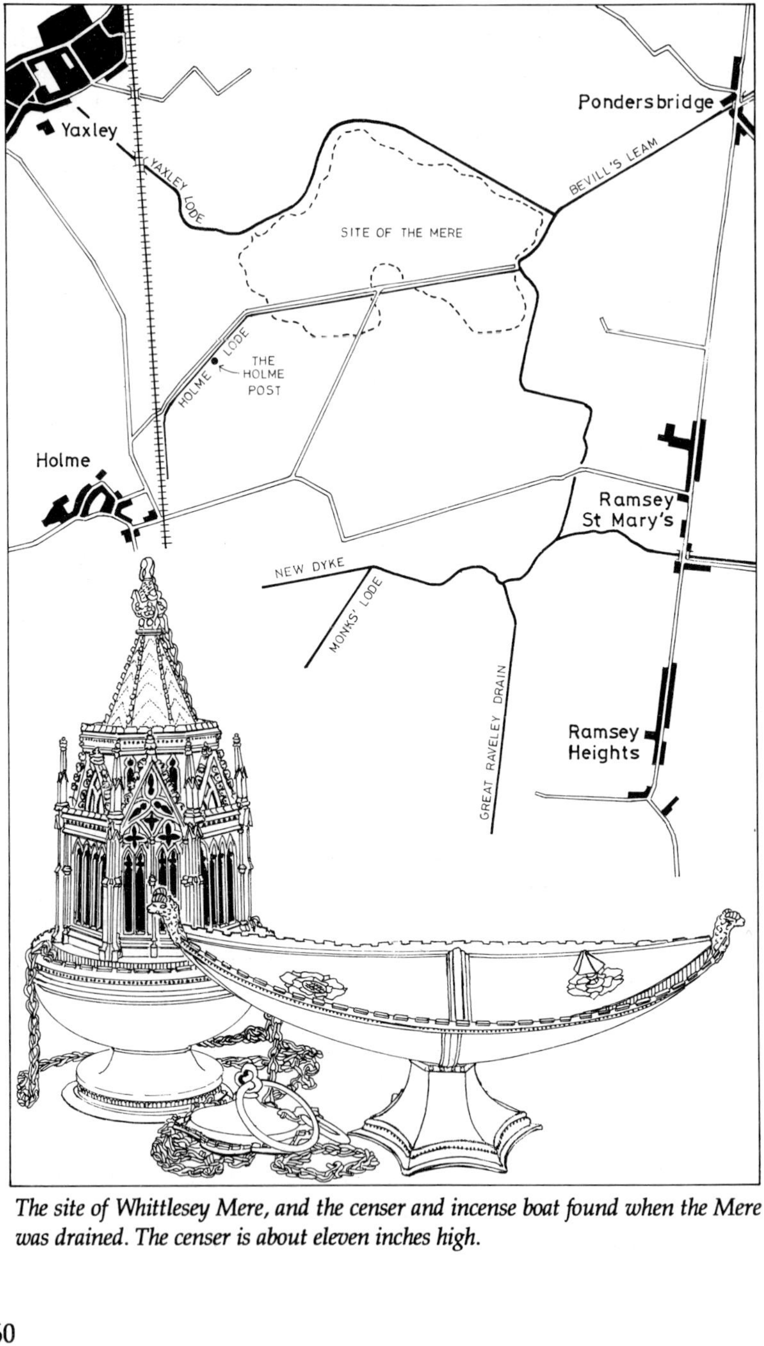

The site of Whittlesey Mere, and the censer and incense boat found when the Mere was drained. The censer is about eleven inches high.

with the sea in prehistoric times.

Draining the Mere had a drastic effect on the wildlife that used to live there. Marsh Harriers, Kites, Bitterns, Ruffs and Spotted Crakes were all recorded as common in the area before the Mere was drained, but vanished soon afterwards. So did the Swallowtail Butterfly, while the Large Copper Butterfly became completely extinct at about the same time (see p.14).

The Tallest Shooting Story

John Heathcote, the squire of Conington Castle, told the following story in the 1860s:

> There are several circumstances worthy of record that took place at the early part of this century in the vicinity of Whittlesey Mere. A Fen man named Bury, worthy of credit, stated that he fired a large duck gun at a flock of snipes that were sitting on Blea Ground, and at one shot killed 36 dozen.

The 'large duck gun' was presumably a punt gun, a huge weapon fired from a boat; its large bore allowed it to fire more than a pound of shot. All the same . . . 36 dozen is 432 birds!

The Oldest House

The Manor House at Hemingford Grey is said to be **the oldest continuously inhabited house in England**. It was built in about 1150 as a fortified manor house, with the front door on the first floor reached by a ladder. The house had a moat round it – probably two moats originally, but the River Ouse has now been diverted through the outer moat.

The house was greatly altered in the 16th century and in the 18th century (when the beautiful Miss Gunnings were born there – see p.25). But when the house suffered a bad fire in 1798, many of these later additions were burned down, while the solid stonework of the original manor house survived.

The children's writer Lucy Boston bought the house in the 1930s and lovingly restored it; she also created the present garden, with its topiary. Her son and his family still live there.

The Shortest Peerage

Henry VIII made one of his favourites, Charles Brandon, the Duke of Suffolk. Suffolk sometimes repaid the king by doing his dirty work for him, and among his services to Henry he visited Buckden Palace to

Hemingford Grey Manor House

bully Catherine of Aragon into admitting that she was no longer Queen of England, and to get her to move to Somersham (see p.11). Catherine resisted his pressure, but Buckden was to have a sinister place in the history of Suffolk's family.

The Duke died in 1545 and was succeeded in the title by his young son Henry. In July 1551 the new Duke of Suffolk, then aged fifteen, was at St John's College, Cambridge with his thirteen-year-old brother Charles. An outbreak of the dreaded 'sweating sickness' at Cambridge caused the brothers to flee to Buckden, but they had left their escape too late and both were taken ill the evening they arrived at the bishop's palace there. The Duke died the same night and his brother about half an hour afterwards. Their tomb can still be seen in Buckden churchyard.

The death of the Duke meant that his brother succeeded to the title and was himself Duke of Suffolk for the few minutes before he died – the shortest tenure of any peerage that has been recorded. The brothers' deaths ended the Brandon family's possession of the Dukedom.

WHAT DO YOU MEAN, YOU DON'T BELIEVE ME?

SOURCES OF INFORMATION

Books

The Victoria History of the County of Huntingdon (three volumes), 1926, 1932 and 1936.

The Dictionary of National Biography

The Complete Peerage

Abell, Francis, *Prisoners of War in Britain 1756–1815*, 1914.

Boston, Lucy, *Memory in a House*, 1973.

Broad, David, *The History of Little Paxton*, 1989.

[Carruthers, Robert], *The History of Huntingdon*, 1824.

Cobbett, William, *Rural Rides*, 1830.

Cowper, William, *Private Correspondence of William Cowper Esq.*, 1824.

Dady, Jack, *Beyond Yesterday. A History of Fenstanton*, 1987; *Hilton, Huntingdonshire*, 1992.

Dunton, John, *The Life and Errors of John Dunton*, 1705.

Edgington, S. B., *The Life and Miracles of St Ivo*, 1985.

Edmonds, Arthur, *A History of Great Gransden*, 1892–95.

Green, H. J. M., *Godmanchester*, 1977.

Jenkins, H. J. K. (editor), *Lord Orford's Voyage Round the Fens in 1774* (revised edition), 1993.

Mee, Arthur (editor), *The King's England. The Counties of Bedford and Huntingdon*, 1939.

Middleton, Paul (editor), *Whittlesea Mere*, 1987.

Newell, Joe, *The Holywell Story*, 1991.

Noble, Mark, *Memoirs of the Protectorate-House of Cromwell*, 1784.

Noble, W. M., *Huntingdonshire*, 1911.

Owen, Roderic and De Vere Cole, Tristan, *Beautiful and Beloved. The Life of Mavis de Vere Cole*, 1974.

Peach, *Flt. Lt.* S., *The Pathfinder Station. A History of Wyton Airfield*, 1984.

Pearse, *Col.* Hugh, *History of the 31st Foot Huntingdonshire Regiment*, 1916.

Pepys, Samuel, *The Diary of Samuel Pepys* (various editions).

Rodger, N. A. M., *The Insatiable Earl: A Life of John Montagu, Fourth Earl of Sandwich*, 1993.

Rowley, Peter, *The Chronicles of the Rowleys*, 1995.

Sadler, S. L., *A Royal Entertainment? Huntingdon August 1645*, 1995.

Saunders, W. H. Bernard, *Legends and Traditions of Hutingdonshire,* 1888.
Sewel, William, *The History of the Rise, Increase and Progress of the Christian People Called Quakers,* 1834.
Tatem, Moira, *The Witches of Warboys,* 1993.
Tebbutt, C. F., *St Neots. The History of a Huntingdonshire Town,* 1978.
Wickes, Michael, *A History of Huntingdonshire* (revised edition), 1995.
Wise, John and Noble, W. M., *Ramsey Abbey, its Rise and Fall,* 1881.
Woodham-Smith, Cecil, *The Reason Why,* 1953.

Periodicals

The Transactions of the Cambridgeshire and Huntingdonshire Archaeological Society, seven volumes, 1904–1952.
The Records of Huntingdonshire (the journal of the Huntingdonshire Local History Society), from 1965 onwards.
The Huntsman (the journal of the Huntingdonshire Family History Society), from 1986 onwards.

Other Sources

The Norris Museum, Huntingdon Record Office and Huntingdon Library have collections of material relating to all aspects of Huntingdonshire.